SO FAR...
A Life Lived for Others

SO FAR...
A Life Lived for Others

David Robles

XULON PRESS

Xulon Press
2301 Lucien Way #415
Maitland, FL 32751
407.339.4217
www.xulonpress.com

© 2021 by David Robles

All rights reserved solely by the author. The author guarantees all contents are original and do not infringe upon the legal rights of any other person or work. No part of this book may be reproduced in any form without the permission of the author.

Due to the changing nature of the Internet, if there are any web addresses, links, or URLs included in this manuscript, these may have been altered and may no longer be accessible. The views and opinions shared in this book belong solely to the author and do not necessarily reflect those of the publisher. The publisher therefore disclaims responsibility for the views or opinions expressed within the work.

Unless otherwise indicated, Scripture quotations taken from the King James Version (KJV)–*public domain*.

Paperback ISBN-13: 978-1-66282-395-4
Ebook ISBN-13: 978-1-66282-396-1

Table of Contents

Introduction vii

Chapter 1: My First Childhood Memory 1
Chapter 2: My Parents 3
Chapter 3: My Family 5
Chapter 4: A Pre-birth Experience 7
Chapter 5: From Boy to Teenager 9
Chapter 6: My Mom's Plight 11
Chapter 7: Facing Reality 13
Chapter 8: I Got Saved! 15
Chapter 9: New Outlook 19
Chapter 10: My Dad's Dilemma 21
Chapter 11: Could No Longer See 23
Chapter 12: A Drastic Occurrence 27
Chapter 13: Day of Decision 31
Chapter 14: My Life Changed 35
Chapter 15: Hitting Rock Bottom 39
Chapter 16: Precious Moments of Divine Appointments 43
Chapter 17: Face to Face with Failure 47
Chapter 18: The Last Three Weeks 49
Chapter 19: Remembering the Unforgettable 53
Chapter 20: Beginning the End 57

Chapter 21: From Darkness to Light 61
Chapter 22: Confirmation of a Miracle 65
Chapter 23: Son, It's My Turn 69
Chapter 24: The Day I Ran 71
Chapter 25: For God So Loved Me... Conviction 75
Chapter 26: See You Later ... Mom 83
Chapter 27: What Am I Doing Now? 87

Conclusion 89

Introduction

WHILE SITTING ON my living room sofa, I had just finished reading a book. A book about a young boy's testimony of how he went from a troubled childhood to a life of purpose and destiny. He attributed his success to God and his older sister, who told him during their family's difficult times that he was born for a special reason. Also, that there was a special purpose for his life. After reading his story, it motivated me to tell many about my own story. After reading his book, it inspired me to write my own book.

What was birthed in me that afternoon has come to pass. This very book that I have written I dedicate to my best friend Jesus Christ, to the memory of my parents, to my brothers and sisters, to every person who has physically cared for another, and to all of those who will one day care for a family member or friend. May God bless all of you with salvation! Also, please receive from me a handshake and hug of appreciation and gratitude for your great service in the area of caregiving.

My First Childhood Memory

I REMEMBER MY FIRST childhood memory very well. It was Monday morning and the first day of a new school year. I was four years old and looking out through the living room window, watching my two older brothers starting their seven-block journey to school. While my brothers were at school, there was really nothing for me to do. My dad would be at work. My two younger sisters were too small for me to play with and that meant my mom would be busy taking care of them. Also, I really wasn't permitted to go outside alone because I was too young to take care of myself. All that was left for me to do was to watch old reruns of old cartoons on our old television. As a result of that, it left me longing for my two brothers to return home from school so that we could go out to the front or backyard to play like always. In those days, my brothers meant everything to me because we were very close. We were a close-knit family because that's what our parents taught us to be.

My Parents

MY PARENTS WERE both born in Mexico. My dad came from a family of eleven, not counting his parents, while my mom grew up as the only child because her two older brothers died very young. They both came from middle-class families, as each family owned their own store. My dad was raised in a "machista" household, meaning he grew up in a male-snobbiness setting. Thus he became what he became: a somewhat cruel but hardworking man who showed his love toward us by working hard at his job in order to provide for our needs.

My mom, being the only child, grew up in a home where she had everything she needed, wanted, and then some. Then, even though her parents divorced while she was about four years of age, she still had everything except for the love of her natural father, which her stepdad could never give her despite being a very good man. What my mom thought was a bad thing, in that she lost her dad because she never saw him again for as long as she lived, turned out to be a good thing for her, my dad, and us in the long run. This event helped change her from a spoiled brat into a woman who would go through anything for the love she had for my dad and us. In other words, my mom became a woman who loved her family like no other woman I have ever seen in my entire life!

My Family

MY DAD WAS forty years old and still single. He had already fathered at least eight kids, two sons, and six daughters that he knew for sure were his. He was single because he never wanted to get married for some reason or another. That same year, he met my mom. As she and her mother walked into his leather shop in Tijuana, Baja California one day, he saw her and said to himself, "That's the woman I want to marry!"

My mom at the time was only sixteen years old and lived in the central part of California. My grandparents didn't approve of their relationship because of the twenty-four-year age difference. That, along with my dad being a man full of pride and somewhat obnoxious in his behavior, caused many disputes between him and my grandparents. Despite the age difference, the arguments, and the 500 miles that separated their homes, they became boyfriend and girlfriend. My dad would drive eight hours one way every weekend just to talk to her for one hour because of good behavior. If he misbehaved, his time would be cut in half, or he would be asked to leave. This went on for six years until they finally got married on my dad's forty-sixth birthday. My mom was like his birthday present. On their wedding day, my dad promised my grandmother that he would give her six grandchildren. In the first four years of their marriage, my parents already had three boys and one girl, in that order, and the relationship between my dad and my grandmother worsened. It got so bad that my grandmother told my mom, "As long as you are married to him, you are not welcomed in my house anymore!" After this, my mom was devastated but knew that her responsibility was to her husband. That same year, Esther was born. She was the fifth child in our family, but the first and only child born with a handicap.

She was diagnosed with mental retardation. In the next ten years my parents had one more daughter and one son, making it four boys and three girls, and a family of nine altogether. Well, my dad fulfilled the promise he made to my grandmother, and us kids grew up without the nurturing of our grandparents while my mom experienced being a wife and mother at a young age without the complete support and guidance of her mother. In other words, she went through all that because of the love she had for my dad. Even though all these things took place, we were considered by many of our family members and friends as a normal and functional family.

A Pre-birth Experience

THERE WAS A pre-birth experience my parents told me about that I never forgot. I remember that day very well. I was about thirteen years old when my mom and dad were telling me the story of how my mom heard me crying while still in her womb. She was startled, and at the same time she was amazed. She felt something strange, as though the child in her womb was going to be somewhat different-perhaps a little special. Afraid of telling my dad, she did anyway, with the condition that he should not tell anybody about it. Well, my dad didn't take it very well. Instead of honoring my mom, he told everyone he came in contact with.

You see, my parents were somewhat religious. We as a family would sometimes visit church, but we were never dedicated in serving God, going regularly to church services, or anything of that nature. In other words, we were not saved by the grace of God! They both believed in the superstition that if a child cried in the womb of his or her mom, that child would have some kind of extrasensory perception of some sort. Perhaps the child would be able to read the minds of people, or even predict the future. God only knows what they really were thinking about.

It did become evident to my mom that my dad really believed in that superstition more than she did. According to him, the only way to prevent that belief from happening was to tell everyone about it. Later in life, my mom found out that he did it out of fear. How did she come to know that?

Well, one day, when I was about three or four years of age, we were eating at the dinner table. Out of nowhere, I told my dad to drink some water. He just looked at me. Then he started to choke on a piece of food, was forced to grab his glass of water and drink to avoid choking. To my mom, it was obvious that my dad didn't want some freak following him everywhere he went telling him, "do this" or "don't do that." This is the story my parents told me.

I, to this day, really don't believe in superstitions, nor am I condoning it in anyway. My mind was on, why I was crying in my mom's womb. Maybe I cried because of the life I was going to live here on earth after birth. Maybe I cried because of the lives of others I was going to meet in life. That question remained with me for a very long time. The one thing that was for sure: as I look back now, the act of helping my dad did make me feel special. Like some kind of superhero.

From Boy to Teenager

As time went on, things were pretty much normal. Before my youngest brother was born, we lived in the south central part of Los Angeles. We called ourselves the Hispanic version of the Brady Bunch because we were three boys and three girls.

Then we moved from Los Angeles to the city of Bellflower. Later, we moved to the city of Whittier, until we finally ended up in the city of Norwalk.

After two months in our new home, my mom gave birth to my youngest brother. Shortly after, my mom was very worried because she really didn't feel any labor pains before, during, or after giving birth like in times past. That, along with an occasional numbness in her hands and feet accompanied with a light degree of pain, caused her to visit her doctor. After many studies, the doctor concluded that my mom had an acute case of degenerative rheumatoid arthritis. His diagnosis was that my mom was supposed to have this infirmity at a later age but, because she accidentally fell flat on her face one day while walking on a sidewalk, it resulted in her having this sickness at an earlier date. In other words, my mom had this infirmity concentrated in one area in the inside of her body. When she fell, the fall caused this sickness to spread throughout her inner body and to manifest itself immediately. The bad fall she suffered happened a little bit before she became pregnant with my little brother.

Before all this, I would rarely find myself assisting my dad and mom in matters that were primarily their responsibility as parents. As it turned out, I was twelve years old and found myself more involved in the affairs of the family than ever before. Whether I knew what was happening or not, whether I understood what was taking place or not, whether I accepted it or not, I was being asked indirectly by my parents to somewhat put my childhood aside. Also, to grow up to face the reality of what was taking place in the life of my mom and how it was affecting my dad and us as a family.

My Mom's Plight

EVEN THOUGH MY mom had arthritis, she continued being a mom to us and a wife to my dad. I didn't know where she got the strength to go forward, but somehow she did. Of course, there were days where it seemed my mom just wasn't around. At times, the pain she suffered was unbearable. Even if she took her prescribed medicine or painkillers, sometimes it wasn't enough.

I remember this one occasion when my mom was in her bedroom, lying on her bed and crying because of the pain she was experiencing. My dad and I were in the living room watching television when we heard her crying out. Right away, my dad told me to follow him. We went into the bathroom where he opened the hot water faucet to the bathtub and quickly started soaking some bath towels. We soaked about three towels. Then we went into my mom's bedroom. There she was crying and at the same time massaging her knees, trying to calm the pain. My dad quickly started wrapping her knees with the soaked towels. At first she cried even louder. I thought the reason she cried out was because the towels were too hot. The more she cried the more my dad continued wrapping her legs with fresh towels as I would go back to re-soak them. Afterwards, my dad told me not to bring anymore towels because my mom stopped crying as the pain wasn't as bad as before. That was the first time I assisted my dad in attending to my mom. As it turned out, it wouldn't be the last.

Later that day, my dad told me that during these times of suffering, my mom had contemplated many times of taking the whole bottle of painkillers and ending it all right there. I was shocked to hear that. Was the pain that strong that she would rather die? Then I realized that the only reason she went through these difficult moments was that the love she had for us was greater and more powerful than any pain she had already suffered.

Facing Reality

IN THE NEXT five years of my life, many things took place. My mom continued having her moments of pain, but this time on a regular basis. This left my dad searching for better doctors and better medications while the oldest of my three sisters practically ended up raising my little brother on her own. Also, our family as a whole went through the physical, emotional, mental, and financial struggles that a family of nine would face in the late 1970s and early 1980s. More than that, we were living under the circumstances of having a mom whom her doctors were nearly labeling as a disabled adult and a father nearing retirement from being a utility man at a major company for thirty-two years.

On an individual basis, I unexpectedly found myself at the age of thirteen working as a gas attendant at a service station. Even though I was a full-time student in the eighth grade, I was working thirty-three hours a week at my job. This I did for fourteen months until I finally quit my job because my grades were dropping from "A"s and "B"s to "D"s and "F"s.

One highlight from working this job was that I was able to spend my money wisely. On numerous occasions, I paid for my dad's car repairs that were done at my job. I also remember taking my mom and three sisters on a shopping spree where I bought them a lot of clothes. Most of all, I was able to save a good part of the money I earned with my dad. He was like my personal bank.

After I quit my job, I found life in general harder than before. In a matter of months, all the money I earned was gone. In school it was an uphill struggle as I had to study harder to get better grades. Also, I started to feel the peer pressure stronger than ever before. I was being pressured into trying drugs, enticed into sexual promiscuity; the influence of joining a gang was overwhelming and that of drinking beer or alcoholic beverages was a norm among us teens. Furthermore, I felt the urgency of having to grow up faster than ever before in order to help my dad carry the family's burdens. At that time, I didn't consider myself as a "mama's boy." I thought of myself more as a "daddy's boy" because for some reason or another, of all my brothers and sisters, he looked to me to help him confront the necessities and crisis that our family was living through.

Of all the incidents that were taking place, the worst of all was that which was happening to my dad. Now in retirement, he started having problems with his eyesight as he began to see less and less.

I Got Saved!

AS I RECALL, I was seventeen years old, and my family that was at one time considered as normal and functional became very dysfunctional as we began to fall apart. My mom, in spite of her illness, still tried her best in caring for Esther and my youngest sister and brother, while the oldest of my sisters was sixteen and getting married the following year. My two older brothers dropped out of high school, one because he was earning good money at his job while the other was experiencing personal problems. Most of all, my dad continued experiencing problems with his eyesight.

All the things happening around me, combined with the personal stuff I was going through, brought me to a place of total frustration.

As a way of escape, I thought that joining the football team and taking my frustrations out on the field would be a good way to let out some steam. After the season, I found myself worse off. About two weeks later, I had reached my boiling point where I couldn't take it anymore.

I remember that day very well. It was the middle of December in the year of 1982. I was in my senior year at Norwalk High School and a teenager who was very mad at the world. I felt so much anger inside me that it started bursting out. I was walking around campus with an old friend of mine. We were talking about school until I finally blew up in a rage of anger. I started kicking over trash cans. I even kicked this one boy in the backside. He turned around wanting to hit me, but when he saw the fury in my eyes he quickly walked away. Then my friend did something I will always remember. He stood in front of me and looked me in the face. Now, I was about six feet tall while he was only five feet and two inches in height. My face was filled with hate while his face had on a gentle smile. Then he pointed his finger to my face while I clutched my fist ready to knock him out with one blow. With boldness, he said the three words that I will never forget in my entire life, "You need Jesus!" I was about to smack him, but when I heard that, I couldn't even move. I was frozen stiff! Right then and there, with the both of us still looking at each other, I started to cry. Then I asked him, "What do I need to do?" He then said, "Receive Jesus Christ as your Lord and Savior." Amazed, I said, "That's all?" To which he replied, "Yes!"

In prayer, I found myself being led by my friend into a new life. I felt like a brand-new person now that I was saved. Right away, all the anger was gone. Perhaps the warmth I felt was God's love that melted the anger while the tears I cried washed it all away. Moreover, in that same moment, I strongly believed that God Himself placed in my heart to one day become a pastor. With that in my heart and mind, I began reading the Bible and telling others of His love.

New Outlook

NOW THAT I was saved, the way I lived my life changed. Before, I lived a life of trying to do all I could, whether it was good or bad to God because my mentality was that I was only going to live once in this life. Now that I understood about going to heaven after death, I started to live a life of doing good deeds to please God. Also, my attitude about helping my parents at home was different. Even though my parents and relatives considered me as a good son or boy, I had an attitude of indifference when it came to helping my family. My attitude then became one of honoring my parents and loving my family because it was good in the sight of God. Furthermore, the biggest change came in the area of not feeling lonely anymore. Despite having my parents, my three brothers, my three sisters, and all the friends from school, I still felt somewhat lonely, as if I were the only one in the world living under these circumstances, facing these situations, and experiencing the life I had been living.

All that changed when Jesus became my new friend. I strongly felt His presence with me, which gave me a lot of confidence to face whatever challenges were in the road ahead. Little did I know that the events that were going to take place in the upcoming years would be of great impact. So dramatic that if I didn't have Jesus in my life, I wouldn't have made it. As I look back to the timing of when Jesus came into my life, I am left to say that His time of arrival was perfect. Yes, He came at the right time!

10

My Dad's Dilemma

SIX MONTHS LATER, I graduated from high school. Including my parents, I was the first in my family to graduate. My parents went to my graduation ceremony and were very proud of me. At this time, life was very good.

After the summer, I decided to continue my education by going to a community college. That's when I made the decision of attending Cerritos College in the city of Cerritos, California. It was only about two blocks from where we lived so it made it very convenient.

A few months into school, my dad became very worried about the condition of his eyesight. He had already started to see less and less. Now he was having a hard time when it came to driving, walking around the neighborhood, and even watching the news on television. As a result of this, he made an appointment with his optometrist, hoping to get a higher magnification on his already prescribed glasses.

When my dad and I got there, right away he was called in by the receptionist. We both entered the examination room. I went in to help translate because my dad really didn't speak English. I watched as the eye doctor examined my dad's eyes using various machines that were there. He did many studies. After an extensive examination, he concluded that my dad had a lot of pressure in his eyes due to either glaucoma or cataracts. Also, he strongly suggested that my dad get a physical to see whether anything was wrong with his health that was indirectly affecting his eyesight. Moreover, he stated that if my dad didn't act quickly, he would eventually lose his eyesight completely. When I heard this, it hit me very hard that I almost passed out. I quickly left the examination room and went straight to the restroom where I threw some water on my face, while ringing in my ears was the phrase, "My dad is going to be blind!" After calming down, I raced back to the examination room where I found my dad very angry and ready to go. I thanked the doctor as we left the office. On our way home, I could see that my dad had mixed emotions about the doctor's diagnosis. Even though he was angry, I could see that there was more fear in him than anything else. Fear of one day going blind.

Now, why was my dad filled with anger and fear? You see, it was instilled in him by his parents and peers that going to a medical doctor was a "sin" before God. A sin because he was placing his faith and trust in a man and not in God. That's the way many people of his generation were taught, and that's the way they devoted themselves to live.

11

Could No Longer See

For the next two years, my dad pretty much tried everything in the book. Everything and anything to recuperate his 20/20 vision, except that of going to a medical doctor for help. We bought certain vitamin supplements that were known to better your vision. He ate certain foods that contained a high volume of vitamin A, hoping a new diet would help him. Also, because of his religious upbringing, he had a jeweler make him a small golden plaque with a pair of eyes engraved on it. This he set at the altar of a certain church in Los Angeles in order to fulfill a ritual. During all this, his condition continued getting worse.

Now apart from seeing less, he started to get nervous, anxious, and fearful. He would get nervous in trying remedy after remedy and ritual after ritual because there were too many out there at the time. His nervousness overtook him where he couldn't drive the family car anymore, so I had to do the driving from that time on. Anxious, because he was hoping that after trying one of these remedies or rituals or a combination of a few or all, his eyesight would be normal again. Overall, he became fearful of the fact that he was going blind. Even though he was trying "his hardest" to regain his vision, no progress was being made.

Then came the day when it was officially declared by my dad that he could no longer see. The oldest of my sisters was already married, and after a few years had passed she had her first son. She came over to visit us and show us her little boy. He wasn't even two weeks old. She placed her son in our dad's arms. Our dad gently and carefully held his first grandson in this family and fixed his eyes on him for awhile. Then my sister took her son to the bedroom to show our mom her first grandson ever. Everybody was excited and happy! As for me, I was very happy about being an uncle for the first time. Then the visit ended as the day was also ending. While everyone was going to turn in after a day of excitement, I found my dad in the kitchen, standing in front of the medicine cabinet. He was just standing there in a very deep thought. I went to him and asked him if he was okay. While closing the cabinet door, he looked toward me. Then he started to cry while telling me how he had his grandson in his arms and, even if he tried his hardest to see him, he couldn't. At that time I couldn't find any words to say, so I ended up crying with him.

God only knows how this affected my family individually and as a whole. All of us kept on going as life just went on. As for me, I had to take on more responsibilities. I became my mom's crutch by helping her walk when we went out. Also, I became my dad's eyes as I would guide him pretty much everywhere we went. Moreover, I became somewhat of a substitute parent to my two sisters and little brother that still remained at home.

12

A Drastic Occurrence

I HAD JUST GRADUATED from Cerritos College with an associate of arts degree in Business Administration with a transfer to a university. Having graduated with a 3.34 grade point average, I considered many universities. Among them were Cal State Long Beach, Cal State Dominguez Hills, Cal State Fullerton, and UCLA, which was my favorite. Overall, my choice was Cal State Fullerton, where I would finish my schooling in order to receive my bachelor's degree upon graduation.

I was now at the university. Right away, I saw a big difference between the college life and the university life. The students there were more into their studies. It was hard making friends because I only saw my classmates during class. After class, it seemed like everyone would disappear. As a result, I was having a hard time adjusting to this life. As time went on, I started to feel I didn't belong there. I would get up every morning and drive sixteen miles to school in my parents' old 1973 Ford LTD, and believe me, that car wasn't in tip-top shape. At school, I could only speak to a few classmates during class. My teachers were no longer called "teachers" but now had the title of instructors. They gave me tons of homework as if there was no tomorrow. Then, at the end of the school day, it was another sixteen miles to return home.

While school was getting somewhat tough, things got worse at home. My mom, needing dentures, was visiting the dentist in order to have all her teeth removed. From the removal of her teeth to the making of her dentures, it took some time. During this time, she wasn't eating well or enough, which caused her to become anemic. Now, having arthritis and being anemic was a deadly match. Like out of nowhere, my mom, who could at the time barely walk, couldn't walk anymore. The anemia caused my mom's arthritic condition to worsen by causing her bones to shrink, leaving her crippled. In other words, it was like she shrunk into herself. She was now slouching over; her arms seemed to be pressed firmly onto her body leaving her with little movement of them, her legs were somehow pressed tightly together as if they were sewn together from the hips to the knees and, worst of all, the arthritic pain became more severe. Just like that, my mom went from walking to sitting on a wheelchair and from standing tall to barely keeping her balance as she tried standing. Also, she went from experiencing a higher-than-moderate level of pain to a severe and excruciating level of pain like never before.

After all this, I thought, What happened? How did all of this come about? The only answer I could come up with was that from the first day my mom was diagnosed with arthritis, she always had the mentality that the slimmer she was, the less pain she would feel. Numerous doctors have told her that the more a person weighed, the more pain that person would feel. Perhaps because she embraced this way of thinking in order to ease or get rid of the pain, it had cost her the ability to walk. Instead of making things better, it made them worse.

13

Day of Decision

AT HOME, MY mom for the last few months wasn't able to cook for herself, much less for my dad and our family. My little brother and sister Esther would both have lunch at their own schools. My baby sister for some reason or another spent much of her sophomore year at home, so our dad would ask her to feed him. She would also feed our mom. My baby sister and I, as a result of our parent's physical· state, would take care of the household chores which involved some cooking, cleaning, laundry, taking out the trash, helping our mom and dad take their showers, and helping them both get dressed. She would dress our mom while I helped our dad. Then I would run some errands like pick up the needed medications at various pharmacies and shop for food, household supplies, and clothing, just to name a few. Along with all this, I still had to find time to do my homework from school. Up until this point, this was my life. Then came a day I never expected. A day I was brought to a place of decision.

I remember that day very well. It was about the beginning of April. My sister Esther, little brother, mom, dad, and I were all in the living room. Except for my dad and little brother, we were all watching television. My little brother, on the other hand, was sitting on the floor playing with his toys. While my dad, sitting about ten feet directly in front of the TV, was listening to his radio. My mom and Esther were to his right and my little brother to his left. I was sitting about three feet from the TV on my dad's right, leaving me pretty much in between my dad and the TV. In other words, my dad was to my left while the TV was to my right. As a result of the TV and the radio being on at the same time and my little brother making his own sound effects while playing with his toys, there was a lot of commotion going on. Then the unthinkable happened!

While I was watching television, I strongly felt my attention being drawn toward my dad. As I turned my head to look toward him, somehow everything around me went into a state of slow motion while the noise dropped considerably. Strange as it may sound, it was as if time stood still. Then I zoomed into my dad and focused on him for what seemed like an eternity. He was looking down and seemed very sad. While observing my dad, I strongly felt God showing me how my dad was in need. The more I looked, the more I felt compassion for him. Then, as I turned my attention back toward the television, everything went back to its normal speed.

After a few minutes had passed, my dad called out to me and said, "David, I am dying of hunger because your mom can no longer feed me!" Wow! I wasn't surprised when I heard that. It was amazing how God prepared me before that moment occurred. Even though I started to ask God for direction on how to answer my dad, I knew deep down inside that the answer was, "Okay, dad, I will help you."

14

My Life Changed

NOW THAT I made the decision to help my family, I needed to make a few changes. Of course, the biggest change of all was that of leaving school. Due to the fact that I received state grants in order to pay for my schooling, I had to finish off the remaining six weeks of the semester. Otherwise I would've left school the very next day.

After the semester, I actually felt excited about being at home seeing to every need that existed and any need that arose. Not including my dad, I would take my family to their appointments whether they were medical, dental, or school related. Also, I was really motivated about taking care of my parents, attending to the household chores, and running all the errands that were necessary. Even though I did all this and then some, I would still go out to the movies with friends, attend sporting events, visit family members, and go to church on Sunday mornings. Since leaving school, this was my life for the next two years until more changes were demanded from me.

As my mom's infirmity was in a controllable phase by the various prescribed medications, my dad's sickness was taking him down a dark and lonely road. In addition to losing his eyesight at the beginning of his diabetic condition, he also had open sores that sprung out through about 40 percent of his body. Primarily around his lower legs, upper back, and upper arms. Also, he had some on his ears, which seemed very strange to me. It was like the sugar in my dad's blood was traveling throughout his body, looking for a way of escape rather than leaving through the traditional bodily functions.

Now that a few years had passed, the open wounds were closed just like my dad's eyes continued to be. As much as he tried to focus his eyes on something, open his eyes as wide as he could, or even cry his hardest, hoping his tears would wash away the blindness, he remained without vision. This brought my dad into a place of depression where he became very sad because he always believed that having the ability to see was the most precious gift anyone can have.

Along with the depression, the levels of nervousness, anxiety, and fear arose dramatically. It got so bad that he would eat up to six or seven small meals a day, drink liquids almost always, go to the restroom more than usual, and instead of sleeping eight-hour shifts, he would sleep or nap about three hours pretty much anytime he needed to. During the time he was awake, he wanted and needed to be attended to, whether it was early in the morning, in the afternoon, or late at night. It really didn't matter much to him. You see, to my dad, day or night didn't exist anymore. It became this one long dark night in a life of just trying to survive. As a result of this, I didn't go out anymore. If I did, it was to run the same errands as before which I did even faster. As for my social outings, they were a thing of the past. I literally cut off all my male and female friends by telling them I was always busy. After a while, they stopped coming over, then stopped calling. Also, the only sporting events I saw were on television. My usual family visitations were terminated. Most of all, I couldn't go to church anymore. My living room became my sanctuary. These things I did because my dad wanted and needed me by his side, primarily just to keep him company. As it turned out, this was the life I lived day after day, week after week, month after month, then year after year. This went on for about five and a half years.

15

Hitting Rock Bottom

During the five and a half years, there were some good times that brought much-needed laughter and joy to our lives, along with many bad times that somehow found a way to erase all the goodness. Also, there were a few victories that brought a sense of purpose in living, despite the hardships we were facing, accompanied with many defeats which primarily served in lowering our self-esteems.

In addition to all of this, my dad experienced a lot of pain, suffering, and agony that drove him to a place of total frustration. Him being in this condition only made things worse. His frustrations later turned into anger and hatred. Against what or whom? Perhaps, against the blindness and/or the diabetes which caused it in the first place. Maybe against the optometrist who told him he was going blind. Could it have been against his own way of thinking or his own beliefs? Then again, was it against himself or, worst of all, was his anger and hatred against God? At that time I didn't know the answer to that question. What I did know was that my dad was taking out some of his frustrations on me. No longer was he asking or telling me to serve him but ordering for things to be done as if he were a mean sergeant from the armed forces during boot camp. Sometimes he would actually yell out his commands! During these difficult times, I could see the anguish in his face. His desire to see again was not being accomplished, leaving him in a place where he was losing all hope in recuperating his vision.

As a result of this, instead of getting together and bearing each other's burdens, this drove my parents further apart. My mom already because of her sickness didn't allow my dad to sleep in her bed. While she slept in her bedroom, my dad found a sense of refuge and security sleeping in the living room. The kitchen and bathroom were easily accessible from the living room, which made it easier for my dad to be accommodated. Also, my dad, by making the living room his place of dwelling, gave him a feeling that he had everything under control, even though most of the time it wasn't like that.

Moreover, with everything that was going on with my parents regarding their relationship or lack of it and their infirmities along with its affects on them as individuals and us as a whole, our family was not just falling apart, but the broken pieces were landing on the ground. As I experienced everything that was taking place, I saw, heard, and felt everything as if I were living it myself. My parents' burdens and frustrations became mine, especially on my dad's part. I found myself burdened, depressed, frustrated, angry, and filled with hatred. It is true, you literally become the person you associate yourself with. As my dad's world came tumbling down, hitting rock bottom, I ended up beside him, lying on that same rocky ground.

16

Precious Moments of Divine Appointments

BEFORE I CONTINUE writing the remainder of this book, I desperately need to add the following accounts in order for a better understanding of the next chapter.

A little after the five-and-a-half-year period started, I remember an incident that took place which at the time didn't seem important. My mom, two sisters, and little brother were in the living room, along with my dad. Everybody was watching television while my dad was lying down on his rollaway bed, facing opposite the TV. I, on the other hand, was alone in the kitchen, preparing something for all of us to eat. As everybody was quietly enjoying the program they were watching, my dad started yelling out, "David, they're coming to take me! They are going to take me!" This he said several times out loud. Due to the fact that the kitchen was next to the living room, only a doorway away, I quickly looked at my dad as I slowly made my way toward him. Right away, I could see he was startled and yelling from the top of his lungs as everyone around him watched quietly. Before approaching my dad, I took my attention off of him to look at my mom. My mom, after seeing my dad, looked at me as I was watching her. She didn't say a word, but her face said it all. It was a mix of indifference and anger, as if she were saying, "All that yelling just for nothing!" Then when she looked down, I focused my attention toward my dad again. When I found myself standing next to his bed, he continued yelling out the same phrases as before. Watching him, I began to feel a deep compassion for him. Not knowing what to say or do, I decided to gently lay my right hand on his upper back. It was a way of letting him know that I was right there with him. With my hand on his back, he stopped yelling. Then, after taking my hand off of his backside, he began to yell out again. This time, in a very angry way, he yelled out, "Why did you touch me? Now, because you touched me, they are not going to take me anymore!" At that moment, I clearly understood that my dad was already fed up with his infirmities and was nearing the point of giving up altogether. My dad actually wanted to go with those whom he referred to as "they."

Then there was another incident which took place about midway through the five and a half years. It was around eight in the evening on a weeknight. My dad and I were alone in the living room, listening to the Dodgers' baseball game on the radio. While we heard the game on the radio, I watched it on television with the volume all the way down. Any plays that my dad heard and didn't understand, I would describe them to him because I saw them played out on TV. This we did every time the Dodgers had a game that was simulcast. I really don't remember whom the Dodgers were playing against, what inning they were in, nor who won the game. What I do remember about that one particular night has stayed with me to this very day.

As always, we were really into the ball game. Even though I would watch the game, sometimes I would look at my dad to see if he was enjoying the game as much as I was. Well, this night he seemed somewhat depressed. As I saw him looking down most of the time and not reacting to the plays with excitement as in the past, I couldn't help but feel sorry for him. Then, as I focused my complete attention toward him, I felt a warm feeling come upon me. The warmth was accompanied by a soft voice which spoke to me with authority. I could hear the voice instructing me to lay my right hand on my dad's eyes. Once my hand was upon his eyes, I was to say, "Receive your sight in Jesus' name!" What I was supposed to say and do was as clear as day. Where the voice came from was also clear to me. It was God Himself who wanted to heal my dad of his blindness through me. Instead of being obedient by following through with the instructions, I just sat there and did nothing. It was the first time this had happened, but it wasn't the last.

A few years would pass and the same scenario would take place. Everything was the same, except that it didn't happen during a baseball game. It happened while I was reading the Bible out loud to my dad. I felt the same feeling, heard the same voice and the same instructions. Again, my failure to respond to the command was the same.

As I look back, now I know that my failure to respond to the voice of God was due to my lack of faith. I thought to myself, "Can God really use me to heal my dad?" Also, when those two incidents took place, fear gripped my heart. I thought, What if I do what I am told to do and it doesn't work? Most of all, I feared and dreaded the fact that my dad was going to get mad at me again. Just like the other time when I touched him while "they" were going to take him. As all of these feelings and thoughts ran wild within me, it left me responding to them instead of obeying the voice of God.

17

Face to Face with Failure

Two chapters ago, in the one titled, "Hitting Rock Bottom," I wrote about how after all the things we went through, my dad and I found ourselves at our lowest points ever. I have heard many times before that when you hit rock bottom, there is nowhere to go but up. Even though I was a firm believer in this saying, something occurred later on that made me change my point of view concerning this statement.

We were in the month of October of the year 1992. During the beginning of this month, I remember confessing to my dad how God had visited me and wanted to heal him of his blindness through me. Most of all, how this had happened twice, and how twice I failed God.

After telling my dad this, I saw his countenance change. He seemed shocked with disbelief that because of my disobedience and lack of faith, he remained without sight. Also, he seemed very heartbroken to know that I was afraid of being used by God to bring healing to him. As if, in his silence, he was telling me, "David, all this time, I thought you really cared for me!" All these thoughts ran wild within me as I saw him looking down after he had heard me completely. Then he looked toward me and simply said, "David, if you don't help me then who will?" Right then and there, I realized how I not only failed God but my dad as well. All this time, before my very eyes, I saw how my dad tried everything in the book and out of it to regain his sight. How he had suffered a variety of things because of his blindness. How he went through everything he experienced waiting for God to heal him. How he would spend his days and nights without end, crying out to God for a miracle. A miracle God answered through me which never got to my dad because of me. At that precise moment, I was left speechless as my heart dropped deeply within me.

As the days passed, I thought about this over and over. Then I began to realize that in reality I failed God, my dad, my mom, and my brothers and sisters. I had failed my whole family! The feelings I felt, knowing that I completely failed everyone, caused me to fall even deeper into a place I have never been before. If I had already hit rock bottom, then I must have slid through the rocks somehow, only to find myself underneath all of them. Crushed by all the rocks that were on me and burdened by the guilt of failing everyone, it seemed as though the weight of all the world were upon me. Being in my deepest point, it wasn't to my surprise to find out I wasn't alone. There next to me, I found my dad. He must have slid through the rocks also.

18

The Last Three Weeks

For the next two weeks or so, everybody seemed to be out and about their own business, while my dad and I were like zombies, barely existing and holding onto whatever we had at the time even though it wasn't very much. The both of us were without any motivation or hope.

During these gloomy days, my dad spent a lot of time on the front porch of the house where he would soak his feet in a thirty-gallon washtub. He would have me fill the tub with water. Also, against my opinion, he wanted me to add a cup or two of some ultra detergent. Out of obedience, I would add this very concentrated detergent to the water while he would massage his feet in the process. In minutes, the water would be very soapy. As I would watch my dad, all that I could think of was that he was doing what he thought or believed to be the best for himself at the time.

Then on the twenty-ninth day of October of the same year, I remember waking up well rested after a night of uninterrupted sleep. Something which I haven't had in years! As I got up, I was waiting for my dad to start asking for something to eat or drink. To take him to the bathroom, outside for another feet-soaking session, or to do whatever he planned for the day. This time it was different. Instead of getting out of bed when I got up, he stayed laying there. Thinking that perhaps my dad didn't hear me, I made some extra noise on purpose. Still, he just laid there. Which left me somewhat perplexed because this wasn't the norm. At the same time, it left me somewhat happy because I had a little bit of freedom which I hadn't experienced in a while. As the day progressed, my dad finally got up and sat on his recliner as always. I asked him if he needed anything, to which he didn't reply all. At that moment, I didn't think it strange because sometimes my dad would wake up in a bad mood. I found myself leaving it at that. Nearing the evening of that day, my dad remained silent. When it came time to turn in at the close of the day, I offered to serve him anything he wanted. The response was the same. As he laid back in bed, I did the same.

The next day was pretty much the same as the day before. Then I started to ask myself, Is my dad on some kind of fast? When the third day slowly came around, I expected my dad to finally break the code of silence. When he got out of bed, he remained quiet and didn't ask for anything at all. Quickly, I thought something is very wrong here! During this time, I noticed the big toe on my dad's left foot was half its normal thickness. Worst of all, it looked like his toe bone was wrapped with a dark-green dried-up thin slab of meat. I didn't know what this was. What I did know was that it wasn't a good thing at all.

Out of a deep concern accompanied by some heartfelt tears, I remember giving my dad a pep talk about the necessity of eating in order to be strong and healthy. My words did have some impact on him because he started to eat and drink again, even though his consumption of nutrients was very sporadic. Instead of hours in between meals like before, he would sometimes spend days in between them. This routine went on for about twenty days, until my dad and I entered into a night I will never forget.

19

REMEMBERING THE UNFORGETTABLE

IT WAS AN early evening on the seventeenth day of November. While my mom and sister Esther were in their bedroom, my dad and I were in the living room as usual.

I remember my dad was lying naked on his bed, covered by a blanket. The reason he wasn't wearing any clothes was because he was running a fever. While he was on his bed, I was sitting on my recliner.

Then my dad sat up and asked me to take him to the bathroom. As I led him there, I was amazed that he had enough energy to walk, even though he rarely ate in the past three weeks. While he sat there, I waited standing next to him. Then he said that he couldn't do anything. Hearing him say that made me break down into tears. With my tears slowly running down my face, I answered my dad, "How can you go to the restroom if you haven't eaten in three weeks?" Then he said, "I want to lie down." I told him, "You can't lie down on the restroom floor!" I gave him my hand so he could stand up, but he didn't have any strength at all to stand. Seeing how he just wanted to lie down, I decided to pick up my dad and carry him to the living room. As I held him around his chest with a bear hug, I made my way to his bed. I could feel his legs dangling from side to side as I walked through the hallway and into the living room. I guess with all the movement and the bear hug I gave him, my dad urinated on my left leg. When we got to his bed, I sat him on it. As I helped him lay down, I could see that he was about twenty pounds lighter from about three weeks ago. I thought no wonder he didn't weigh so much when I carried him. He was already slim, but now he seemed to be under a hundred pounds. After I covered him with his blanket, he seemed almost lifeless laying there. Right away, I ran to the bathroom to wash my leg with soap, water and some rubbing alcohol. There was a strong odor that accompanied my dad's urine. It smelled like rotten meat. After washing my leg, I quickly changed my clothes, then I went back to the living room.

As I entered the living room, my dad heard me and called me to him. When I approached him, he told me, "David, get me up!" Being already in tears, I answered my dad with my voice already starting to break down. I asked him, "Why do you want to get up when I just barely laid you down?" As soon as I said that, I heard an inner voice tell me to be obedient to my dad. As I helped him on his feet, I placed my hands under his armpits in order to help him stay standing. While his arms rested on my shoulders, we found ourselves face-to-face. Then he slowly dropped his head to look down and said something that astounded me. He said, "God, I am ready ... take me." As my crying intensified, I helped him lay back down on his bed. As that phrase played over and over in my head, I found myself just sitting down close by, waiting to see what was going to happen next.

At that moment, it seemed like my dad and I were the only two people in the whole world. My mom or sister Esther didn't call on me for any assistance, nor did they come out of their room for anything. Also, the phone didn't ring, nor did anybody come knocking on our front door. As my dad and I were in the living room, our own little sanctuary, it was like time stood still ... again.

A few hours had passed. The sun gave in, allowing the moon to rise and give off its lesser light. The quietness from the room of my mom and sister gave evidence that they were now asleep, while I found myself still sitting down on my recliner, ready to face whatever was to take place. I had made the decision that I was going to be by my dad's side even to the end. After I made that decision, that is when the beginning of the end began.

Beginning the End

MY DAD, WHILE lying down, began to toss and turn, showing a lot of discomfort. I got a chair and sat next to the head of his bed, giving me the ability to watch, talk, and hear him closely. Right away, I saw him opening and closing his mouth, as if he were chewing on something. Concerned, I asked him, "Dad, why are you doing that?" He didn't answer me. Then he started to vomit. He was vomiting this thick dark-blue mucus-like liquid. I took his pillow in order to wash the pillowcase and put on a clean one, this time placing a hand towel over the pillow just in case he would vomit again. I found myself replacing the hand towels often and washing the dirty ones in the washer. When I sat next to him, he asked for a drink. I could barely understand him because his voice sounded muffled, as if he was drowning in his vomit or his throat was really drying up. I gave him something to drink. There I saw how he had a hard time swallowing the water I gave him. From that moment on, everything began to happen at a faster pace. It unfolded into a vicious cycle of tossing and turning, vomiting and cleaning up the mess, and of running back and forth to the washer, then back to my dad.

When I sat there next to my dad again, everything seemed to calm down tremendously. Before I knew it, many hours had raced by faster than the speed of light. It was already a little after six in the morning. I found myself very hungry and tired because about twenty-four hours had gone by without me eating or sleeping.

Sitting there, I began to really look at my dad. As my eyes filled with tears, I started to think about the idea of my dad passing on. Also, about the two times I failed praying for him. I thought if my dad were to die right then, I wouldn't be able to live with myself! Then, by the grace of God, I felt his presence again, clearly understanding that He was giving me another opportunity. Hungry, tired and emotionally drained, I mustered up everything I had within me, along with every bit of courage I had. Then, under the unction of God, I rapidly placed my right hand on my dad's forehead and with authority said, "In Jesus' name, receive your sight!" Quickly, as I took my hand off of him, my dad swung at me saying, "Don't touch me!" Right there, I knew for sure that he not only wanted to go, but that his departure was a sure thing.

It was now 6:45 in the morning, and knowing there was really nothing else I could do, I moved my bed next to his, leaving only his recliner in between them. Then, after all the wear and tear of the day, I decided to lie down. Covering my whole body with my blanket prevented me from smelling the odor of the vomit that filled the living room. Also, it gave me a place to pray to God. I told God that I was leaving my dad in His hands because there was nothing else I could do. Plus that I was going to sleep as well as my dad and that we were going to wake up the next day different people.

From Darkness to Light

THE SOUND OF what seemed like a spoon or fork falling into the kitchen sink woke me up from my sleep. As I took off the blanket from over my head, I felt like a huge weight was lifted from my shoulders. Right away, I knew that my dad was now … gone. I looked at the clock to see what time it was. It was 10:45 in the morning. Suddenly I stood up and went over to my dad's bed. There he was, without any life at all. He was lying on his back as his head was facing straight up. I leaned over in order to see his face up close. Staring at him for just a while, I noticed his left eye was closed while his right eye was wide open. As I watched my dad, not one tear came from my eyes. Not because

I didn't care. It was because I had cried so many times for him that I didn't have anymore tears to shed even if I wanted to.

With my mom and sister Esther still in their bedroom, I called my older brother and told him that I needed to speak with him. When he came over, I told him that our dad had passed on. Also, that I needed him to go and bring over our two sisters and little brother. I told him not to tell them anything until we were all gathered together. With his complete attention focused on me, I could see he was deeply moved, but at the same time he was calmly listening to my instructions. After I was done speaking, quietly and quickly, he left.

Meanwhile, I went into the kitchen to grab something to eat as I waited for my family to come over. After a few minutes, the oldest of my sisters came in. She went straight to our mom's bedroom after making eye contact with me. I could see she didn't know what was going on. Then a few more minutes had passed when my baby sister came in. Upon entering, she saw me and quickly looked down while making her way to our mom's bedroom. Seeing her reaction, I knew that our older brother told her what was going on. Then my older brother came in and told me that he couldn't find our little brother.

Now with our mom and three sisters in the bedroom, my older brother and I were in the kitchen. I told him because he is older than me, it was his responsibility to inform the family. Right away, he went to our mom's bedroom while I stayed in the kitchen. Instead of taking his time breaking the news, he just entered the room and, within seconds, I heard everyone scream. Then everyone made their way to the living room, including our mom whom was in her wheelchair. They all gathered around dad. Hugging, kissing, and crying over his lifeless body. Seeing all of this made me cry for the first time since my dad's departure.

After all the commotion, I called all the authorities. While waiting for their arrival, we called the oldest of our brothers, who lived near Sacramento at the time, to inform him about dad.

When the paramedics and police arrived, they all came in and saw that my dad's body was already in the rigor mortis stage. Looking closely, the police saw his naked body covered only by a blanket, the visible gangrene on his left foot, and some old scars and bruises that accompany untreated diabetes. Seeing all this, one of the two officers turned to me and said, "You know what we are thinking about here, right?" I looked at him and said, "Yes, sir, elder abuse." He said, "Yes!"

Right there I quickly thought, Am I going to jail just for helping my dad all these years? Also, I am going to jail even after all these things we went through! Without saying a word, I just looked at the officer with a look of, "Well, here I am, ready to be taken in." That's when my mom spoke out and said, "It was his decision, not ours, of not receiving any medical help!" With the testimonies of my mom, sisters, brothers and self, they were completely convinced that this wasn't a case of elder abuse. The police concluded that my dad was a man who wanted to be healed by God and not by another human who called himself "doctor."

We were on the 18th day of November in the year 1992. I remember very well waking up at 10:45 in the morning. That meant that my dad passed on sometime between 6:45 a.m. to 10:45 a.m. In between those four hours, my dad left his world of living in darkness and entered a new world where he would now live in the "light." Greater still was what God revealed to me about what took place during those four hours my dad was alone with Him.

Confirmation of a Miracle

AS I REMEMBER images of how my dad was facing up with his left eye closed and his right eye opened and how I prayed for the healing of his blindness, God revealed to me something awesome. He instilled in my heart and mind the very fact that my dad, before passing on, received his eyesight again! Yes, my dad was healed of his blindness by God through me! It was as clear as day. There was no doubt at all within me that his one and only desire in the latter part of his life of seeing again, God gave it to him. At that moment, I received it and proclaimed it all by faith as a miracle. A miracle that God would confirm took place through another miracle seven years later.

It was in the summer of 1999. Our church in Norwalk, California sent a missionary team to Guadalajara, Jalisco in Mexico. We were to take part in a five-day crusade, evangelizing the city for Christ. We opened the crusade with a live drama. Then for every night after that, we had special music, prayer sessions, and the preaching of God's Word, accompanied by altar calls for salvation. Literally hundreds were being healed, delivered, and saved in the first three nights we were there.

Apart from this mission, my friend Jorge and I had another mission we set out to accomplish. We were to visit and evangelize the family members of another friend I had in Norwalk. My friend had family in Guadalajara, Jalisco and Zamora, Michoacan, which was about two hours from Guadalajara. During the crusade, we visited my friend's family. There were about twelve members that we met and, after evangelizing, led to God's salvation.

After the service on Wednesday night, Jorge and I focused our attention in going to Zamora. Facing some opposition, we both knew that our trip was urgent. We already knew that we were going to meet some of my friend's family, supposedly around fourteen members more. Most of all, we were going to meet my friend's grandmother who was blind because of diabetes. At that moment, I didn't completely realize what was taking place or what could take place. I just knew that she was blind because of diabetes just like my dad was before he passed away.

A few hours later, we finally made it to Zamora. We met all fourteen members of the family, including the grandmother who was not only blind, but her right wrist was heavily bandaged due to a fall she had a few days earlier. Later we began to evangelize, which led to the salvation of every member that was present. Then I sat next to the grandmother as I elaborated of what salvation meant. Sitting next to her, I began to ask her a few questions. I told her to face me. Then I asked her if I had a mustache or not, which at the moment I did. After following the sound of my voice, she focused all of her attention toward me and said, "I really can't say because I can't see you." Quickly, I signaled to Jorge to start praying silently. Then I explained to everyone there about praying to God for their grandmother, how we can now unite as children of God and pray together for the healing of their grandmother. I then stood up and placed my hands on her blind eyes. Then, out loud, I told everyone to start praying for a miracle. They were to pray to God from their hearts for their grandmother's healing in the name of Jesus. With everyone praying, I began to pray out loud. At that moment, I felt an authority, boldness, and unction come upon me like never before as I prayed for her. Afterwards, as I said amen, everybody repeated amen with me.

Then I sat back down next to the grandmother and started explaining what we just did as a group; that of praying in unity as the family of God all in the name of Jesus. As I was explaining this, I noticed the grandmother was looking toward every direction. Quickly, she started speaking with a voice of amazement, which caused everybody's attention to be rapidly focused on her. While looking up, she said, "I can see the light!" Then looking at me she said, "You do have a mustache and you're kind of chubby!" Wow! God healed the grandmother of her blindness! Some were crying of joy while others were in shock or totally amazed of the miracle they had just witnessed.

After all the excitement, it was now time to sleep. Jorge and I were totally blessed and filled with joy because God used us for the miracle He performed. Then, I thought, we forgot to pray for her wrist. Oh well, we'll pray for her wrist in the morning.

When morning came, she came to us waving her right hand in the air. With great joy and gratitude she said, "When you two prayed for the healing of my eyes, God healed my wrist also!" It was awesome! God, not just healed her eyes, but her wrist as well. Right then and there, God showed me that when He performs a miracle, He does a complete job altogether.

Even greater still was how I heard God on my insides saying, "The same miracle I did here was the same miracle I performed on your dad!" God was confirming with the miracle in Zamora the miracle He performed in Norwalk seven years earlier! Just like God answered the prayers of this grandmother, He answered the prayers of my dad as well! Wow, God is an amazing God indeed!

23

Son, It's My Turn

NOW THAT MY dad was gone, I thought my job as a caregiver was over. I was a twenty-seven-year-old youngster who was ready to go out anywhere I wanted to, make new friends, work a job, go back to school, get married and, if possible, go back to church. I was now free to fly like an eagle, soaring for days without end to any destination and spend any amount of time I wanted. All these thoughts ran wild within me, until one day I looked at my mom in a different light.

A week after my dad left, my mom and I were in the living room, talking about life after dad. As I heard my mom speak, I could tell she was indifferent when it came to following my dad or staying here for the sake of our family. Then, my mom, understanding that her husband was now in heaven, her countenance changed where she became determined to stay here for her children. Despite her infirmities, she was going to press forward and finish her job as a mother. Then I asked her, "Mom, remember you said that if you were in dad's position, you would let me go to live my life?" After I said that, she looked at me for a few seconds. Then she slowly tilted her head down. Seeing her reaction was no surprise to me. I asked her that question, already knowing what her response was going to be. Furthermore, when I asked her that question, I knew for sure that my job or mission as a caregiver was not over yet.

For all of us, life without dad was different. My life was now somewhat easier. Taking care of mom, Esther, and watching over my little brother was easier than I thought. Sometimes we would go out together. Then there would be times I went out alone.

Even though I had some liberties, somehow it wasn't enough for me. I guess all the wear and tear of the past was now taking its toll. Consequently there would be times I just felt like running away from it all!

24

The Day I Ran

WE WERE NOW in October of the year 1993. I was a part-time supervisor for a small company in a nearby city. By this time, I was searching for a way to obtain my complete independence because I had been struggling very much between fulfilling my calling as a caregiver and being independent.

Then, at work one day, a man came in to apply for a job. While he was speaking to my boss, I could easily hear their conversation. She wanted him to work certain hours during the day and some at night. Then he said that he couldn't work those hours because he went to church almost every night. When he said that, something jumped inside me. Right away, I felt that I needed to speak with him. I wanted to find out what church he went to. After they concluded their interview, I called him over and asked him what church he attended. Quickly, he pulled out a small flyer and gave it to me. He told me they were having a church service tomorrow. I told him I would be there. When he left, I started to read the flyer. In big bold letters it read, "Jesus is the answer!"

The next day, I went to church where I had a tremendous time! I even rededicated my life to God, which was awesome. For the next year I sporadically went to church, which was a mistake on my part because I continued to struggle even more with wanting to be completely free. In other words, I didn't want any commitments at all.

Then came an opportunity to go on a two-week vacation to Mexico City, Mexico. Two of my friends and I were to drive all the way from Norwalk, California to Mexico City. I arranged for my mom, Esther, and little brother to be taken care of while I was gone. Therefore, I had purposed in my heart that I was going to go and have some good clean fun because I knew that many opportunities to do the opposite were going to confront me. Most of all, I didn't want to mess up my life nor my renewed relationship with God.

It took us fifty-four hours to get there. Being in Mexico City was great because I was now experiencing the freedom I always wanted. I was having such a great time that I didn't want to go back home. My two-week vacation became three weeks. Then it became four weeks. Before I knew it, I was going on my twelfth week in Mexico. My family back home wanted me back because they missed me and were experiencing problems that only I could help them with.

Well, after three months of being in Mexico, I went back home. At that moment, I didn't know that my vacation wasn't a vacation at all. It was an excuse so I could run away from it all. From my commitments, job, and above all, God and the calling He gave me of helping my family. I literally ran away from everything and everybody I knew, including ... God.

For God So Loved Me...
Conviction

FINALLY, AFTER THREE months of having good clean fun during my getaway, I was now back home. I was received by my family whom were somewhat bothered because of the length of my stay in Mexico. Also, I found them needing my assistance in the caring of our mom, Esther, and little brother. I was only gone for ninety days, and in that time my brothers and sisters experienced firsthand that my position as a caregiver was no simple task.

Even though my stay in Mexico was one of relaxation, it wasn't enough rest from working five and a half years straight at home with my family. Now that I had tasted freedom, I desperately wanted some more. Therefore I purposed in my heart that the next time I stepped on Mexican soil, I was going to live it up! In other words, the next time I found myself in Mexico, I was going to do whatever I wanted, even if it was considered bad in the eyes of man or God. The reason I thought this way was because I felt that my days of being a caregiver were going to be forever. Then the day came when I had to return to the US/Mexico border to cancel the permit we obtained for the vehicle we used on our trip to Mexico. It was Friday morning, the sixth day of January of the year 1995. My friend and I made plans to leave early the next day. Our trip was to take about five hours at the most, which left me arranging everything at home to be taken care of during my absence. As the day went on, the excitement about going on our excursion grew by the minute.

It grew to the point where I didn't think about anything else. Even though I spent all of the day anticipating the fun I was expecting to have on our trip, I felt a very strong need in attending the church service that night.

Later that night, I found myself in church. I don't remember the songs that were sung during praise and worship. I don't remember the petitions that were made during prayer. Nor do I remember what pastor spoke or what the sermon was about. What I do remember was that I spent the whole time there contemplating on the numerous things that could take place the next day. As uncertain as they were, I was ready to do anything and everything I wanted.

Then, during the altar call, I felt a very strong conviction that came upon me. Right away, I knew it was God! It was like He was saying, "David, what are you doing?" After I understood that, I slowly dropped to my knees and prayed a prayer that I had never prayed before in my entire life. I told Him, "God, I know that You love me, and because

You do, I know You are going to correct me. I have always been afraid of Your correction, but I need it very much. Also, I know that after You correct me, You are going to be there for me. Thank You! In Jesus' name I pray. Amen.'" For God so loved me that He brought me to a place of conviction! As a result of this, I was able to pray that prayer.

Correction

After my friend picked me up early the next day, we headed to the border. In what seemed like three blinks of an eye, we found ourselves there. To my surprise, the process to cancel the car's permit was fast and easy. As we walked out of the office through the doors, I said out loud, "I am back in Mexico!" Without any hesitation, I looked at my friend and told him, "Let's head toward Ensenada, Baja California!" Smiling, he replied, "Let's go!"

While we were heading toward Ensenada, I felt like a roaring lion going after its prey. A hungry lion indeed that had been caged for about eight years and finally had been set free. As I was driving down the highway, my heart raced with anticipation. Plus there was a passion in my spirit, a hunger in my eyes, and an excitement that ran through my veins. Therefore I was cutting the curves in order to drive faster. Before I knew it, I found myself speeding down that road toward my own destruction while not caring for anything or anyone. No, not even myself. All I knew was the faster I drove the quicker I was going to have "my fun." In fact, I thought to myself that nothing was going to stop me now! That was my mentality, until God came into the picture.

The freeway we were on was a two-lane highway with one lane on each side going opposite directions. I was driving at about 60 mph going into an S-curve which went under a bridge and continued downward.

As I approached this curve, my friend noticed that I wasn't slowing down. When we looked at each other, I could tell that he wanted me to slow down a bit, which left me responding by continuing at the same speed.

Suddenly from under the bridge came out a two-trailer cement truck driving on both sides of the road, leaving us with no place to go. When the trucker saw us approaching him at a high speed, all he could do was to blow his horn. Very rapidly, as we approached him, I made the quickest and sharpest left turn ever without stepping on the brakes. So sharp, that it was a miracle of God that we weren't hit by the truck, nor did we flip over onto our right side and over the guardrail to who knows where. As I avoided contact with the truck, we found ourselves off the road and onto a loose gravel shoulder. There I stepped on the brakes as hard as I could, and held on to the steering wheel, guiding the car straight forward. Not having complete control of the car's destination, we came to a complete stop when the right front corner of the car hit the corner of the bridge. The impact was so hard that huge chips of cement fell from the bridge.

Once we came to a stop, my friend and I ran out from the left side of the car, expecting it to explode because of any gasoline leaks combined with any sparks. After a few minutes, we knew that any explosion wasn't going to take place. When we got to the car, we saw the damages. The right front wheel was pushed back all the way to the front door of the car. Both tires on the right side were flat. The car would no longer start up. When I looked underneath the car, I noticed the motor dropped to the ground. Most of all, I noticed my friend was hurt. He had twisted his left ankle and really couldn't walk. Then I noticed my left index finger was swollen and it was starting to hurt. Also, at impact, my seatbelt hit my chest then ran up scraping my neck, leaving my skin with a burning sensation. After all this, my friend told me that if the Mexican Federal Police were to pass and see us, we could be thrown into the Mexican jail, which according to him was no place for an American to be. Hearing that, I quickly took off the license plates of the car along with the VIN plate. Then I tried moving the car by pushing it, which was an impossible thing to do because the dropped motor was anchoring the car to its place. Also, the two flat tires didn't help much either. When everything else failed, we decided to just start walking, leaving the scene of the crash.

Once we started to leave, the federal police pulled up beside us and asked, "Where do you guys think you're going?" Looking at both of us with license plates in hand, he continued to say, "Are you guys trying to run away from the scene of the crime?" We were, 100 percent busted! My friend, being a Mexican citizen said, "David, it is best if you stay out of this and let me do all the talking, okay?" Heeding his advice, I found a big rock and decided to sit down on it while he talked to the police.

While sitting upon that big rock, I started to pray to God. As I prayed, I felt His overwhelming presence. Right there and then, I knew that this crash was no accident at all. It was God's correction upon my life. Understanding that, I started to cry for joy. Joy because God demonstrated His love for me through His correction. Also, as I sat upon that big rock, I felt God telling me, "David, I will not leave you nor forsake you." Then I realized that God was with me. After looking down at the rock I was sitting on, I looked up and said, "Isn't He the Rock that upholds me?"

All this took place in a small city called, "La Mission" in Baja California, Mexico. The Spanish name of "La Mission" literally translated means "The Mission." That day God had a mission, a mission of love that involved correcting me. For God so loved me that He brought me to a place of correction.

Restoration

Well, there I was. While my friend continued to talk to the police officer, I continued sitting upon that big rock, praying to God. After He showed me His love, I began to really break down on the inside, which led me to ask for His forgiveness. Also, I told Him that if He wanted me to pay for my friend's car, to pay for the damages to the bridge, and to go to jail, I would do all that. In other words, I was going to totally surrender my life to Him by leaving myself completely in His hands.

After praying, I began to see the restoration of God starting to work in my life. My friend arranged with the police officer for me not to be taken to jail and not to pay for the damages to the bridge. Also, the officer arranged for us to be taken to the nearest town and for the car to be towed there as well. All this in exchange for the Pioneer speakers, the Kenwood stereo, and all the money I had in my wallet which was forty dollars.

As we were given a ride to the nearest town by the tow truck driver, I started to take notice of what kind of highway we were on. On many places where there was a guardrail, it was there to prevent anyone from going off the cliff and into the Pacific Ocean some two thousand feet below. With that understanding, I really began to thank God because my friend and I should have been dead.

Once we got to the location where the tow truck came from, we told him that the car was now his in exchange for the ride he gave us. Therefore, we grabbed our belongings which included my large windbreaker and about three hundred audio cassettes of various musical artists and/or groups. I used my jacket as a large bag in order to carry all of the cassettes. Afterwards, we asked the driver which direction was the border. Then we started our journey back home on foot.

There we were, walking on the shoulder of the same highway we were driving on earlier. I was holding my jacket full of cassettes with my left hand while my right hand was holding up my friend because he really couldn't walk due to his twisted ankle. Looking around, I saw a taxi coming our way. Not having any money, I remembered about the ring I had in my pocket. It was a golden Jewish-style ring that my older brother gave me about two days earlier. When I signaled to him, he pulled up beside us. Showing him the ring, I asked, "Can you take us to the border?" With his bulging eyes focused on it, he answered, "Hop in!"

Within minutes, we were approaching the border. Before getting there, my friend asked, "How are we going to get home?" Looking at him, I answered, "Don't worry, just keep on paying attention to everything that is happening." As we were pulling up to park, an older couple saw us. When we made a complete stop, the man opened our door and with some tickets in his other hand said, "I have two bus tickets to the city of Huntington Park, California." Then he added, "Do you want them?" To which I replied, "Sir, I don't have any money, but I'll give you this jacket full of 300 cassettes!" Without hesitation, he looked at all the cassettes and said, "Okay!"

At the bus stop located at the border, we had about a two hour waiting period before our departure. My friend and I were now very tired and very hungry. We saw places to eat everywhere we turned to look, but we were flat broke. Then I remembered having some money hidden in the little pocket of my jeans. Quickly, I checked my pocket and found $1.98 in change. With this amount, I went to the nearest lunch truck, bought a meal, and split it between the both of us. When it came time for our departure, we both quickly boarded the bus. As the bus left the border and headed north, we found ourselves in the United States. While on our way home, we were in pain because of our injuries. Also, we were utterly exhausted. Despite all of this, we were glad about almost being home.

Arriving at Huntington Park, we called another friend who picked us up and took us both home. At home, I greeted my family, who were very happy to see me alive and well. Then I went to bed.

While lying on my bed, I replayed over and over all the things that happened from the moment God convicted me to the moment He brought me home safely. From His conviction upon me, to His correction toward me, and all the way to His restoration of me. I was so overwhelmed that for the next eleven days, that was all I talked about. Then, on the 18th of January, I looked up to heaven and said, "God, didn't You convict, correct, and restore me?" After I said that, God filled me with a fire, zeal, and a love for Him like never before!" Most of all, He filled me with the power of His Holy Spirit! For God so loved me that He brought me to a place of restoration.

26

See You Later ... Mom

NOW THAT I was restored, I was completely set free from all my bad habits. Also, I began to attend every church service and every church function there was. Moreover, I began to take my mom and Esther to church with me. Now that they were going to church, they also rededicated their lives to the Lord.

Then in the summer of 1996, we started to attend all the church services that were held in Spanish. By this time, we were attending church and/ or church functions everyday except for Mondays. As a result, I became a better caregiver than ever before because I knew that there was great reward in what I was doing. Actually, I found myself serving my family "as unto to Lord."

In the next three years or so, I became involved in many of the church's ministries in which I led many to the Lord. Also, by the examples of my mom, Esther, and myself combined with our prayers, my two sisters with their families, my three brothers with their families, and our grandmother got saved. Except for our grandmother, we were all going to the same church as one big happy family.

During all this time, my mom still suffered from her acute arthritic pain and from having brittle bones due to osteoporosis. At times, her pain was so intense that her medication wouldn't help her at all. Despite all of this, she would still attend church faithfully.

As we were nearing the year 2000, a very precious moment took place in the life of my mom. While my mom and Esther were in their bedroom, I was in the living room watching television. Then my mom yelled out calling me to the bedroom. When I got there, I could see she was somewhat excited. She asked me what it was like to feel the presence of God come upon me. I told her it was like a rush of joy that brought a feeling of peace in the insides. After hearing my explanation, her eyes lit up while she said, "Wow, it feels so beautiful!" This same scenario would take place two more times in the months to come. Following the third time, my mom told me, "David, I am no longer afraid of dying." Now this was coming from a lady who was absolutely terrified about even thinking of the word death, much more talking about it. Looking at her, I responded by saying, "Mom, that is a good thing." Little did I know that God was preparing my mom for her departure.

It was on a Saturday afternoon, the 5th day of February of the year 2000. My mom had already been a week in the hospital due to excruciating pain because her body was literally shutting down. Surrounded by family and friends, she started sliding very slowly into eternity. In fact, the doctor was so amazed that she was leaving so slowly. Then at 2:45 in the afternoon, my mom left to be with the Lord. A little before her passing away, I remember very well how she whispered very softly into my ear telling me, "I want to go home now."

My mom had finished her race! Fulfilling her ministry as a wife by continuing the work that my dad left her of caring for her children. Also, fulfilling her ministry as a mother by praying for the salvation of her children and seeing it come to pass, thus receiving the promise of God which my dad began in motion when he gave his life to Jesus before passing away. The promise of if you believe, then you and your household shall be saved.

Sunday morning, the very next day, we went to church. During worship, I remember looking up at the television screen, reading the words to the song, "Can't Nobody," as I sang it. Then, as I sang the part about, "He touched and healed me so I ran," I saw a vision above the screen. In the vision, on the left side, I saw my mom standing on her own two feet and without a wheelchair. On the right side, I saw two men standing. One man was behind the other. Without a doubt, I knew the man standing in front was Jesus. Behind Him, I saw my dad looking over Jesus' shoulder toward my mom. When my mom saw my dad, she smiled, but when she saw Jesus, she ran to the both of them. At that moment, I remember saying within myself, "See you later ... mom."

What Am I Doing Now?

NOW, AS I look back, I find that everything I have experienced has happened for a reason. God truly is a Master Builder and Architect of the lives of His children. I can clearly see how the past is really helping me in the present, when it comes to servanthood. Currently, apart from helping in the care of my sister Esther and working as a real estate agent/realtor, my life continues to be one of a servant as I serve others as unto to the Lord through the various ministries at the church I still attend. These are some of the things I do on a daily basis: Mondays, I help teach a home Bible study in Spanish in the city of Norwalk; Tuesdays, I serve as a Spanish interpreter in our Celebrate Recovery meeting where we help the Spanish-speaking communities overcome various addictions, bad habits, and complexes; Wednesdays, I serve as a Spanish interpreter where I translate our English sermons into Spanish for our Spanish-speaking individuals attending our English church services; Thursdays, I serve in various ministries during our Spanish church service; Fridays, I attend our prayer central, where we all get together as a congregation to pray for all the needs of the church and its ministries; Saturdays, I serve as a monitor in our BEAT program (Building Excellence and Achievement in Teens), helping troubled youth with their academics. Also, later that day, I serve as an usher in our 180 West program, a program providing a safe haven for the youth and young adults to experience good clean fun at no cost to them; Sundays, again I interpret for one of our English Sunday morning services and then serve at our Spanish Sunday afternoon church service. This is what I do and will continue to do if the Lord wills it.

Conclusion

WELL, SO FAR it has been a life lived for others. A life of commitment with fulfillment, of sacrifice with honor, of suffering with purpose, of solitude with a great sense of belonging, and of service with satisfaction. In other words, a life based on 1 John 3:16 which states, "Hereby perceive we the love of God, because He laid down His life for us: and we ought to lay down our lives for the brethren"(KJV).

Even though I have experienced all the things I have gone through, I still consider myself blessed and very fortunate in having lived this life. That's why I look at my life as a gift from God designed especially for me, and I wouldn't trade it for anything in this world. For God, through this life of servanthood, has given me an inner joy that will be eternal.

Of this joy I am always reminded of every time I see a very young girl helping her elderly grandmother cross the street. An older gentleman who takes his wife, who is confined to a wheelchair, out for some fresh air. A young individual carrying the grocery bags of an older person to their car. Also, when a stranger takes the time to guide a young blind person onto a bus and so on and so forth.

www.ingramcontent.com/pod-product-compliance
Ingram Content Group UK Ltd.
Pitfield, Milton Keynes, MK11 3LW, UK
UKHW022222230426
12048UKWH00016BA/1010